SNOW LEOPARDS

STUDYING
SECRETIVE
ANIMALS
IN THE WILD

by Joyce Markovics

CHERRY LAKE PRESS

Published in the United States of America by Cherry Lake Publishing Group
Ann Arbor, Michigan
www.cherrylakepublishing.com

Reading Adviser: Marla Conn, MS Ed., Literacy specialist, Read-Ability, Inc.
Content Adviser: Katey Duffey
Book Designer: Ed Morgan

Photo Credits: © Stayer/Shutterstock, cover and title page; © freepik.com, TOC; © Katey Duffey, 4; © Warren Metcalf/Shutterstock, 5 top; © Snow Leopard Conservancy, 5 bottom; © Katey Duffey, 6–7; © Jeannette Katzir Photog/Shutterstock, 7; © Fabio Nodari/Shutterstock, 8; © Gypsy Picture Show/Shutterstock, 9; © Abeselom Zerit/Shutterstock, 10; © chbaum/Shutterstock, 11 top; © andamanec/Shutterstock, 11 bottom; © Jeannette Katzir Photog/Shutterstock, 12; © Karen Kane-Alberta, Canada/Shutterstock, 13; © Josef_Svoboda/Shutterstock, 14; © Christopher Anderzon/Shutterstock, 15; © Dennis W Donohue/Shutterstock, 16; © Katey Duffey, 17; © Gary Koehler, SLT/SLCF, 18; © Örjan Johansson, 19; © slowmotiongli/Shutterstock, 20; © Kwadrat/Shutterstock, 21; Eric Kilby/Wikimedia Commons, 22; Wikimedia Commons, 23; © Katey Duffey, 24; © Katiekk/Shutterstock, 25; © Warren Metcalf/Shutterstock, 26–27; © Steve Wilson/Shutterstock, 28; © CEPTAP/Shutterstock, 29; © freepik.com, 31.

Library of Congress Cataloging-in-Publication Data

Names: Markovics, Joyce L., author.
Title: Snow leopards / by Joyce L. Markovics.
Description: First edition. | Ann Arbor, Michigan : Cherry Lake Publishing, [2021] | Series: On the trail: studying secretive animals in the wild | Includes bibliographical references and index. | Audience: Ages 10 | Audience: Grades 4-6
Identifiers: LCCN 2020030353 (print) | LCCN 2020030354 (ebook) | ISBN 9781534180505 (hardcover) | ISBN 9781534182219 (paperback) | ISBN 9781534183223 (ebook) | ISBN 9781534181519 (pdf)
Subjects: LCSH: Snow leopard—Juvenile literature.
Classification: LCC QL737.C23 M2739 2021 (print) | LCC QL737.C23 (ebook) | DDC 599.75/55—dc23
LC record available at https://lccn.loc.gov/2020030353
LC ebook record available at https://lccn.loc.gov/2020030354

Printed in the United States of America
Corporate Graphics

CONTENTS

A GHOSTLY FIGURE

Zoologist Katey Duffey knelt down to examine fresh tracks in the snow. It was April 2017. The jagged mountains of western Mongolia towered behind her. She placed her hand next to the tracks to **gauge** their size. Excitement filled her body. The tracks belonged to a snow leopard! Katey had been studying the mysterious cats since 2014. But she had never actually seen one. That was about to change.

Zoologist Katey Duffey's hand next to a snow leopard paw print

One evening, while driving through a snowy valley, Katey's teammate saw something move on a mountain slope. They quickly stopped. "Immediately I jumped to that side of the vehicle to see what he saw," remembers Katey. Then she spotted the "ghostly figure of a smoky-gray big cat leaping from one boulder to another."

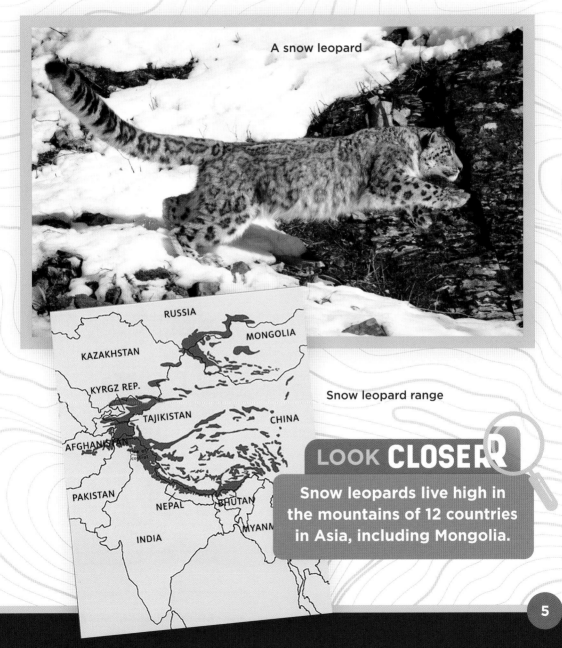

A snow leopard

Snow leopard range

RUSSIA
MONGOLIA
KAZAKHSTAN
KYRGZ REP.
TAJIKISTAN
CHINA
AFGHANISTAN
PAKISTAN
NEPAL
BHUTAN
MYANM
INDIA

LOOK **CLOSER**

Snow leopards live high in the mountains of 12 countries in Asia, including Mongolia.

BIG CAT CALLING

What stood out to Katey was the animal's extremely long tail and powerful leap. But it was too late in the day to get a closer look. Katey wanted to be certain it was the animal she was looking for. So the next morning, she and her teammates returned to the spot where they had seen the creature. "Sure enough, fresh tracks were right where we saw the cat," says Katey. She had seen her first snow leopard in the wild!

Katey Duffey in Mongolia

Snow leopards and other big **carnivores** have fascinated Katey since she was a child. "They are some of the most recognized, yet misunderstood **species**," explains Katey. She knew she wanted to spend her life studying them. "Their power and valuable role in an **ecosystem** drew me in. I just couldn't, and wouldn't, imagine anything else."

LOOK **CLOSER**

Snow leopards are related to other big cats, such as tigers, lions, and jaguars.

MYSTERY
ANIMAL

Studying snow leopards in the wild, however, would not be easy. The animals are often called "ghosts of the mountains" because they're so hard to find. Snow leopards are shy, mostly live alone, and are well **camouflaged**, says Katey. These carnivores also live in one of the most extreme environments in the world—the steep, snowy mountains of Asia.

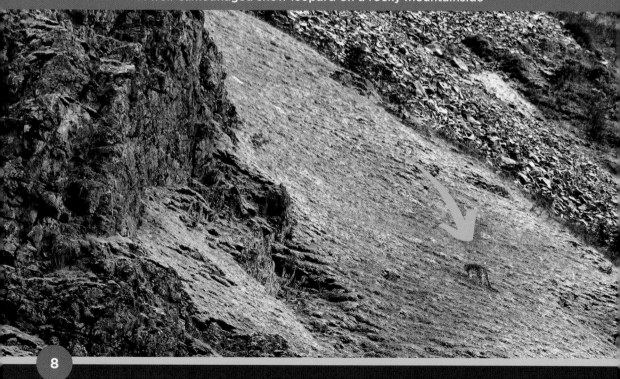

A well-camouflaged snow leopard on a rocky mountainside

Snow leopards make their homes at **elevations** between 10,000 and 17,000 feet (3,048 and 5,182 meters)! They prowl along steep cliffs and rocky slopes. These sure-footed cats have pale gray or creamy colored fur with dark patches called rosettes. The patterned fur helps them blend perfectly into their snowy, rocky home. This makes them even harder for scientists to locate and study.

LOOK CLOSER

Snow leopards have been seen at the base of Mount Everest, the tallest mountain in the world!

Each rosette on a snow leopard has a unique pattern—like a fingerprint!

MOUNTAIN LIVING

What's incredible about snow leopards is that they're perfectly adapted for cold mountain living. They have dense fur up to 5 inches (13 centimeters) thick to keep them warm. They have extra-long, furry tails "to wrap around themselves," says Katey. And the hair on snow leopards' bellies is extra thick to "protect them as they walk through deep snow."

A snow leopard uses its tail almost like a blanket.

There's also fur on the bottom of snow leopards' huge paws. These paws act like snowshoes, helping the cats walk in deep snow without sinking. The animals' big, furry paws "allow for a more effective grip on steep rock faces" too, according to Katey.

An up-close look at a snow leopard's paw

LOOK **CLOSER**

Snow leopards have large nostrils that help warm the cold air before it reaches their lungs.

SNOWY
ATHLETES

Getting around their steep mountain home is no problem for snow leopards. They're some of the best climbers and jumpers in the animal world! The cats have short front legs and strong chest muscles. This allows them to jump as far as six times their body length! Snow leopards can also leap up to 20 feet (6 m) high. The cats' long tails help them balance as they jump.

Snow leopards are able to move quickly and easily up or down a cliff.

Each snow leopard has its own territory, ranging from 18 to 50 square miles (47 to 129 square kilometers). The cats are active mostly in the early morning and evening.

These spotted leopards are powerful hunters too. They can take down **prey** up to three times their size! Like other large cats, snow leopards first **stalk** their prey. Then they pounce with **explosive** speed, grabbing hold of their victim with sharp, curved claws. With a deadly bite, they sink their sharp teeth into their prey.

This snow leopard is eyeing its prey.

APEX PREDATORS

Snow leopards are one of the top, or apex, predators in their **habitat**. Wild goats, called ibex, and wild sheep are their main food. They also rely on smaller prey, such as birds, hares, and marmots. "The presence of the big cat indicates a healthy ecosystem," says Katey.

Snow leopards most often eat meat but will occasionally eat plants.

Sometimes, the number of marmots in an area dramatically increases, leading to **overpopulation**. Snow leopards help keep marmot numbers at a healthy level. In winter, however, marmots **hibernate**. Then hungry snow leopards sometimes prey on domestic animals, including goats and sheep. This creates problems for local herders. "Snow leopards threaten the livelihoods of herders when they kill **livestock**," says Katey.

Marmots are plant-eating rodents that make underground homes.

LOOK CLOSER

In one year, a scientist reported a snow leopard eating: 25 marmots, 15 birds, 9 hares, 5 domestic goats, 5 wild sheep, and 1 domestic sheep!

TRACKING

To better understand the feeding habits and behaviors of snow leopards, Katey spends a lot of time tracking them. She says the best time to study the big cats is during the winter. "Snow makes finding tracks easier," she says. However, winters in the mountains of snow leopard habitat are frigid. Temperatures can drop to –40 degrees Fahrenheit (–40 degrees Celsius)! That's so cold it can hurt to breathe.

After putting on many warm layers, Katey and her teammates head out. "Our **objective** is to find as many snow leopard signs as possible," says Katey. In the mountains, she looks for **scat**, tracks, and any other evidence of leopards. Scat can tell her a lot about the diet and health of an animal. She also sets up and checks video cameras. The small cameras are set up in places where the animals might go. Any movement triggers them to record.

LOOK **CLOSER**

Back at camp, Katey checks the cameras. She hopes for good snow leopard images. But she often finds hundreds of "livestock selfies"!

COLLARING CATS

Scientists also gather important data about snow leopards by capturing live animals. With the help of hidden cameras and leg **snares**, they're able catch the cats without harming them. Once a snow leopard is caught, it is given a drug that safely makes it sleep. Scientists first check the animal's health by weighing and measuring it, and by taking samples of its blood.

Scientist Örjan Johansson collaring a snow leopard

LOOK **CLOSER**

Scientist Örjan Johansson has been collaring snow leopards for over a decade. He has safely collared over 30 cats.

Then the snow leopard is fitted with a special collar and released. The collar allows scientists to track the animal's location once every few hours. Using the information collected, scientists can learn the size of a cat's territory and how often it hunts, for example.

This snow leopard is wearing a collar. After about a year and a half, the collar breaks apart and falls off the cat.

LEOPARD FAMILIES

By studying snow leopards in the wild, Katey and other scientists have learned that males and females **mate** in late winter. To find one another in their rugged mountain home, the cats leave signs. They scrape rocks and trees with their claws. And they leave urine or scat for other cats to find. Snow leopards also make special sounds, such as moans and yowls, to attract a mate.

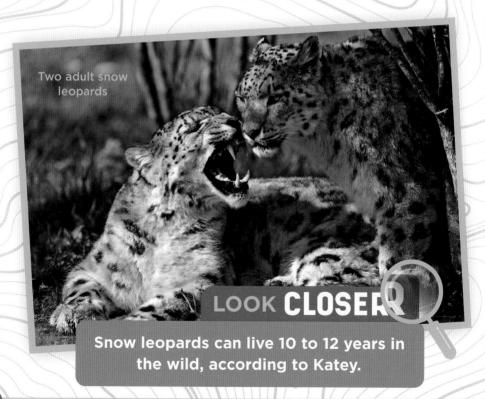

Two adult snow leopards

LOOK **CLOSER**

Snow leopards can live 10 to 12 years in the wild, according to Katey.

After mating, females usually give birth to two or three cubs in summer. The cubs are unable to see when they're born. Their eyes open after about seven days. The babies are covered in dark spots that develop into rosettes. At two months old, they can eat solid food, run, and play. The cubs start learning how to hunt at three months of age. They stay with their mom for up to two years—or until they're ready to live on their own.

Snow leopard cubs

THREATS TO SURVIVAL

There are only about 4,000 to 6,500 snow leopards left in the wild. As an endangered species, the cats are at serious risk of dying out. **Climate change** is a big threat to snow leopard survival. Higher temperatures can force the cats to move up the mountains where it's cooler. However, there's less food at higher elevations. This drives the cats to look for other sources of food, such as livestock.

A snow leopard on the hunt

Another huge threat to snow leopards is hunting. As humans spread out, their livestock become easy prey for leopards. Herders will kill snow leopards that attack their animals. "One of the most effective ways to protect snow leopards is to actually help herders protect livestock," says Katey.

LOOK **CLOSER**

Snow leopards are also hunted for their beautiful, spotted fur and body parts. It's thought that poachers kill hundreds of the cats each year.

Proper fencing helps protect livestock from snow leopards.

CONSERVATION

An important part of Katey's job is working with local herders in order to help save snow leopards. She interviews them to find out how many animals they've lost to snow leopard attacks. She also asks about their "attitudes toward snow leopards." By listening to and working with the herders, Katey hopes to address their concerns while also saving snow leopards. "Conservation starts with education," she says.

Katey interviews a herder inside his home in Mongolia.

Katey partners with different snow leopard organizations and experts around the world. One group is the Snow Leopard **Conservancy**, which formed in 2000. The organization works in seven different countries to preserve snow leopard habitats. The group also creates programs to help herders and educate children about the rare, powerful cats.

Educating children about snow leopards can help protect the animals in the future.

LOOK CLOSER

The Snow Leopard Trust and Panthera are two other groups that help protect snow leopards. They work closely with the communities that share the cats' habitat.

MUCH WORK REMAINS

Katey understands there is still much to learn about snow leopards. "It feels good knowing I'm helping to add even a little bit more knowledge on such a mysterious predator," says Katey. Her goal, however, "is to further understand these powerful creatures and how people can coexist with them."

One day, Katey hopes that more people will know about the critical role snow leopards play in the ecosystem. She also wishes that leopard poaching would come to an end. Without more action, the **majestic** snow leopard might truly become a ghost of the mountains.

LOOK CLOSER

An important way to help snow leopards is to spread awareness about them.

FAST FACTS

SNOW LEOPARDS

Scientific Name
Panthera uncia

Physical Description
Pale gray or cream-colored fur with dark rosettes

Size
3 to 4 feet (0.9 to 1.2 m) long, from nose to rump

Weight
60 to 120 pounds (27 to 54 kilograms)

Main Diet
Wild sheep, ibex, and marmots

Habitat
Mountains of Central and South Asia

Life Span
Up to 12 years in the wild

DID YOU KNOW?

- A snow leopard's tail is almost as long as its body!

- The word *uncia* in *Panthera uncia* means "ounce." Ounce is another term for snow leopard.

- Snow leopards have pale gray or light green eyes.

- These big cats do not roar—rather they yowl, purr, or hiss.

- Snow leopards are more closely related to tigers than to common leopards.

GLOSSARY

camouflaged (KAM-uhf-lahzhd) blended in with one's surroundings because of the colors and markings on one's body

carnivores (KAR-nuh-vorz) meat-eating animals

climate change (KLYE-mit CHAYNJ) global warming and other changes in weather

conservancy (kuhn-SUR-vuhn-see) an organization dedicated to protecting wildlife or the environment

ecosystem (EE-koh-sis-tuhm) a community of animals and plants that depend on one another to live

elevations (el-uh-VAY-shunz) areas of height above sea level

explosive (ik-SPLOH-siv) related to a sudden increase in something, such as speed

gauge (GAYDJ) to estimate or determine the size of something

habitat (HAB-ih-tat) the natural home of an animal or plant

hibernate (HYE-bur-nate) to go into a sleeplike state during periods of cold weather

livestock (LIVE-stahk) animals raised by farmers or ranchers, such as sheep and goats

majestic (muh-JES-tic) having great power and beauty

mate (MATE) to come together to have young

objective (uhb-JEK-tiv) an aim that a person is working toward

overpopulation (oh-vur-pop-yuh-LAY-shuhn) the condition in which the number of animals or people in a place is too great to be sustained

poachers (POH-churz) people who hunt illegally on someone else's land

prey (PRAY) an animal that is hunted by another animal for food

scat (SKAT) body waste from an animal

snares (SNAIRZ) traps made to catch animals

species (SPEE-sheez) a group of similar animals that can reproduce with each other

stalk (STAWK) to track and follow something

territory (TER-ih-tor-ee) an area of land that is lived in and defended by an animal

zoologist (zoh-AH-luh-jist) a scientist who studies animals

READ MORE

Esbaum, Jill. *Snow Leopards*. Washington, D.C.: National Geographic, 2014.

Landau, Elaine. *Snow Leopards*. New York: Enslow, 2010.

Montgomery, Sy. *Saving the Ghost of the Mountain*. New York: Houghton Mifflin, 2012.

LEARN MORE ONLINE

Encyclopedia Britannica: Snow Leopard
https://www.britannica.com/animal/snow-leopard

San Diego Zoo: Snow Leopard
https://animals.sandiegozoo.org/animals/snow-leopard

Snow Leopard Conservancy: Take the Snow Leopard Quiz!
https://snowleopardconservancy.org/kids-page

Snow Leopard Trust: Key Snow Leopard Facts
www.snowleopard.org/learn

INDEX

ABOUT THE AUTHOR

Joyce Markovics has written more than 150 books for young readers. She's wild about rare and unusual animals and is passionate about preservation. Joyce lives in an old house along the Hudson River in Ossining, New York. She would like to thank Katey Duffey for her contribution to this book and for caring deeply about snow leopards and other large carnivores.